50 Smoothie Bowl Recipes for Home

By: Kelly Johnson

Table of Contents

- Classic Strawberry Banana
- Tropical Mango Pineapple
- Berry Blast (Mixed Berries)
- Green Detox (Spinach, Apple, Cucumber)
- Blueberry Pomegranate
- Peach Passionfruit
- Banana Almond Butter
- Chocolate Avocado
- Raspberry Coconut
- Orange Creamsicle
- Kiwi Lime
- Watermelon Mint
- Cherry Vanilla
- Spinach Berry
- Peanut Butter Banana
- Turmeric Mango
- Beetroot Berry
- Cucumber Melon
- Mango Basil
- Strawberry Kiwi
- Apple Pie (Apple, Cinnamon, Oats)
- Pineapple Ginger
- Carrot Cake Smoothie
- Mixed Citrus (Orange, Grapefruit, Lemon)
- Raspberry Lemonade
- Chocolate Cherry
- Avocado Matcha
- Blueberry Lavender
- Cranberry Orange
- Banana Chai
- Spinach Mango
- Honeydew Lime
- Berry Beet
- Mango Turmeric
- Vanilla Fig

- Strawberry Rhubarb
- Pumpkin Spice
- Pineapple Jalapeño
- Coconut Lime
- Chocolate Raspberry
- Almond Date
- Green Tea Pear
- Plum Ginger
- Blackberry Basil
- Strawberry Shortcake
- Peach Raspberry
- Blueberry Cardamom
- Mango Mint
- Cherry Almond
- Raspberry Hibiscus

Classic Strawberry Banana

Ingredients:

- 1 cup fresh or frozen strawberries
- 1 ripe banana
- 1/2 cup plain or vanilla yogurt (or dairy-free alternative like almond milk or coconut yogurt for a vegan option)
- 1/2 cup milk (dairy or non-dairy)
- 1 tablespoon honey or maple syrup (optional, depending on sweetness preference)
- Ice cubes (optional, for a colder smoothie)

Instructions:

1. Wash the strawberries and remove the stems. If using fresh strawberries, consider slicing them for easier blending.
2. Peel the ripe banana and break it into chunks.
3. In a blender, combine the strawberries, banana chunks, yogurt, milk, and sweetener (if using).
4. Blend until smooth and creamy. If the smoothie is too thick, add more milk gradually until you reach your desired consistency.
5. Taste and adjust sweetness if needed by adding more honey or maple syrup.
6. Optionally, add a handful of ice cubes to make the smoothie colder and more refreshing.
7. Blend again briefly to incorporate the ice.
8. Pour into glasses and serve immediately. Enjoy your classic Strawberry Banana smoothie!

Tropical Mango Pineapple

Ingredients:

- 1 cup frozen mango chunks
- 1 cup fresh or canned pineapple chunks
- 1 ripe banana
- 1/2 cup coconut milk (or any milk of your choice)
- 1/2 cup orange juice
- Optional: 1 tablespoon honey or agave syrup (for added sweetness, if desired)
- Ice cubes (optional, for a colder smoothie)

Instructions:

1. Ensure that your mango chunks and pineapple chunks are frozen if you want a chilled smoothie.
2. Peel and slice the ripe banana.
3. In a blender, combine the frozen mango chunks, pineapple chunks, banana slices, coconut milk, and orange juice.
4. Add the optional sweetener (honey or agave syrup) if you prefer a sweeter smoothie.
5. If you want a thicker consistency, you can add a handful of ice cubes to the blender.
6. Blend all the ingredients until smooth and creamy. If the mixture is too thick, add a bit more coconut milk or orange juice to thin it out.
7. Taste the smoothie and adjust the sweetness or consistency according to your preference.
8. Once blended to your liking, pour the smoothie into glasses.
9. Garnish with a slice of pineapple or mango if desired.
10. Serve immediately and enjoy your refreshing Tropical Mango Pineapple smoothie!

Berry Blast (Mixed Berries)

Ingredients:

- 1 cup mixed berries (such as strawberries, blueberries, raspberries, and blackberries)
- 1 ripe banana
- 1/2 cup plain Greek yogurt (or yogurt of choice)
- 1/2 cup almond milk (or any milk of your choice)
- 1 tablespoon honey or maple syrup (optional, for added sweetness)
- Ice cubes (optional, for a colder smoothie)

Instructions:

1. Wash the mixed berries thoroughly and remove any stems or unwanted parts.
2. Peel the ripe banana and break it into chunks.
3. In a blender, combine the mixed berries, banana chunks, Greek yogurt, almond milk, and sweetener (if using).
4. If you prefer a thicker smoothie, you can add less almond milk initially.
5. Optionally, add a handful of ice cubes to the blender for a colder and more refreshing texture.
6. Blend all the ingredients together until smooth and creamy. If the mixture is too thick, add more almond milk gradually until you reach your desired consistency.
7. Taste the smoothie and adjust the sweetness by adding more honey or maple syrup if needed.
8. Once blended to perfection, pour the Berry Blast smoothie into glasses.
9. Garnish with a few whole berries on top for an attractive presentation.
10. Serve immediately and enjoy your delightful Berry Blast (Mixed Berries) smoothie!

Green Detox (Spinach, Apple, Cucumber)

Ingredients:

- 1 cup fresh spinach leaves
- 1 green apple, cored and chopped
- 1/2 cucumber, peeled and chopped
- 1/2 lemon, juiced
- 1-inch piece of fresh ginger, peeled (optional)
- 1 tablespoon chia seeds (optional)
- 1 cup water or coconut water
- Ice cubes (optional, for a colder smoothie)

Instructions:

1. Wash the spinach leaves, green apple, and cucumber thoroughly.
2. Core and chop the green apple, and peel and chop the cucumber.
3. If using ginger, peel a small piece and chop it into smaller chunks.
4. In a blender, combine the fresh spinach leaves, chopped green apple, chopped cucumber, ginger (if using), and lemon juice.
5. Add chia seeds for extra fiber and omega-3 fatty acids (optional).
6. Pour in water or coconut water to help with blending and to achieve the desired consistency.
7. Optionally, add a handful of ice cubes for a colder smoothie.
8. Blend all the ingredients together until smooth and well combined.
9. Taste the Green Detox smoothie and adjust the flavor by adding more lemon juice if desired.
10. Pour into glasses and serve immediately.
11. Enjoy your nutritious and refreshing Green Detox smoothie packed with greens and fruits!

Blueberry Pomegranate

Ingredients:

- 1 cup frozen blueberries
- 1/2 cup pomegranate arils (seeds)
- 1 ripe banana
- 1/2 cup plain Greek yogurt (or yogurt of your choice)
- 1/2 cup almond milk (or any milk of your choice)
- 1 tablespoon honey or maple syrup (optional, for added sweetness)
- Ice cubes (optional, for a colder smoothie)

Instructions:

1. Ensure that your blueberries are frozen for a chilled smoothie.
2. Remove the arils (seeds) from the pomegranate. You can do this by cutting the pomegranate in half and gently tapping the back of the fruit with a spoon over a bowl to release the seeds.
3. Peel the ripe banana and break it into chunks.
4. In a blender, combine the frozen blueberries, pomegranate arils, banana chunks, Greek yogurt, almond milk, and sweetener (if using).
5. If you prefer a thicker consistency, start with less almond milk and add more as needed during blending.
6. Optionally, add a handful of ice cubes to the blender for a colder and more refreshing texture.
7. Blend all the ingredients together until smooth and creamy.
8. Taste the smoothie and adjust the sweetness by adding more honey or maple syrup if desired.
9. Once blended to your liking, pour the Blueberry Pomegranate smoothie into glasses.
10. Garnish with a few extra blueberries or pomegranate arils on top for presentation, if desired.
11. Serve immediately and enjoy this vibrant and antioxidant-rich smoothie!

Peach Passionfruit

Ingredients:

- 1 cup frozen peach slices (or fresh peaches if available)
- Pulp of 2 passionfruits (or about 1/4 cup passionfruit juice)
- 1 ripe banana
- 1/2 cup plain Greek yogurt (or yogurt of your choice)
- 1/2 cup almond milk (or any milk of your choice)
- 1 tablespoon honey or agave syrup (optional, for added sweetness)
- Ice cubes (optional, for a colder smoothie)

Instructions:

1. If using fresh peaches, slice and freeze them in advance for a chilled smoothie.
2. Cut open the passionfruits and scoop out the pulp into a bowl. Alternatively, use ready-made passionfruit juice.
3. Peel the ripe banana and break it into chunks.
4. In a blender, combine the frozen peach slices, passionfruit pulp (or juice), banana chunks, Greek yogurt, almond milk, and honey or agave syrup (if using).
5. Adjust the sweetness and thickness by adding more or less almond milk according to your preference.
6. Optionally, add a handful of ice cubes to the blender for a colder and more refreshing texture.
7. Blend all the ingredients together until smooth and creamy.
8. Taste the smoothie and add more sweetener if desired.
9. Once blended to your liking, pour the Peach Passionfruit smoothie into glasses.
10. Garnish with a slice of peach or a few passionfruit seeds on top for presentation, if desired.
11. Serve immediately and enjoy this tropical and delightful Peach Passionfruit smoothie!

Banana Almond Butter

Ingredients:

- 2 ripe bananas
- 2 tablespoons almond butter
- 1 cup almond milk (or any milk of your choice)
- 1/2 teaspoon vanilla extract
- 1 tablespoon honey or maple syrup (optional, for added sweetness)
- Ice cubes (optional, for a colder smoothie)

Instructions:

1. Peel the ripe bananas and break them into chunks.
2. In a blender, combine the banana chunks, almond butter, almond milk, vanilla extract, and honey or maple syrup (if using).
3. If you prefer a thicker smoothie, start with less almond milk and add more as needed during blending.
4. Optionally, add a handful of ice cubes to the blender for a colder and more refreshing texture.
5. Blend all the ingredients together until smooth and creamy.
6. Taste the smoothie and adjust the sweetness by adding more honey or maple syrup if desired.
7. Once blended to your liking, pour the Banana Almond Butter smoothie into glasses.
8. Optionally, drizzle a little extra almond butter on top for added flavor and presentation.
9. Serve immediately and enjoy this delicious and satisfying smoothie packed with banana and almond goodness!

Chocolate Avocado

Ingredients:

- 1 ripe avocado
- 2 tablespoons cocoa powder (unsweetened)
- 1-2 tablespoons honey or maple syrup (adjust to taste)
- 1 cup milk of your choice (dairy milk, almond milk, or any other milk alternative)
- 1/2 teaspoon vanilla extract
- Ice cubes (optional, for a colder smoothie)

Instructions:

1. Cut open the ripe avocado, remove the pit, and scoop out the flesh into a blender.
2. Add cocoa powder, honey or maple syrup, milk, and vanilla extract to the blender.
3. If you prefer a thicker smoothie, use less milk initially and add more as needed during blending.
4. Optionally, add a handful of ice cubes to the blender for a colder and thicker texture.
5. Blend all the ingredients together until smooth and creamy.
6. Taste the smoothie and adjust the sweetness by adding more honey or maple syrup if desired.
7. Once blended to your liking, pour the Chocolate Avocado smoothie into glasses.
8. Optionally, top with a sprinkle of cocoa powder or grated chocolate for garnish.
9. Serve immediately and enjoy this luscious and satisfying Chocolate Avocado smoothie as a nutritious treat!

Raspberry Coconut

Ingredients:

- 1 cup frozen raspberries
- 1/2 cup coconut milk (canned for a richer flavor, or carton for a lighter option)
- 1/2 cup plain Greek yogurt (or yogurt of your choice)
- 1 tablespoon honey or maple syrup (optional, for added sweetness)
- 1/2 teaspoon vanilla extract
- Ice cubes (optional, for a colder smoothie)

Instructions:

1. Place the frozen raspberries, coconut milk, Greek yogurt, honey or maple syrup, and vanilla extract in a blender.
2. If you prefer a thicker smoothie, start with less coconut milk and add more as needed during blending.
3. Optionally, add a handful of ice cubes to the blender for a colder and more refreshing texture.
4. Blend all the ingredients together until smooth and creamy.
5. Taste the smoothie and adjust the sweetness by adding more honey or maple syrup if desired.
6. Once blended to your liking, pour the Raspberry Coconut smoothie into glasses.
7. Optionally, garnish with a few fresh raspberries or shredded coconut on top for presentation.
8. Serve immediately and enjoy this delicious Raspberry Coconut smoothie packed with fruity and tropical flavors!

Orange Creamsicle

Ingredients:

- 1 cup orange juice (freshly squeezed for best flavor)
- 1 ripe banana
- 1/2 cup Greek yogurt (plain or vanilla)
- 1 tablespoon honey or maple syrup (optional, for added sweetness)
- 1/2 teaspoon vanilla extract
- Ice cubes (optional, for a colder smoothie)

Instructions:

1. Peel the ripe banana and break it into chunks.
2. In a blender, combine the orange juice, banana chunks, Greek yogurt, honey or maple syrup (if using), and vanilla extract.
3. If you prefer a thicker smoothie, use frozen banana chunks or add a handful of ice cubes to the blender.
4. Blend all the ingredients together until smooth and creamy.
5. Taste the smoothie and adjust the sweetness by adding more honey or maple syrup if desired.
6. Once blended to your liking, pour the Orange Creamsicle smoothie into glasses.
7. Optionally, garnish with a slice of orange on the rim of the glass or a sprinkle of orange zest on top.
8. Serve immediately and enjoy this delightful and nostalgic Orange Creamsicle smoothie! The combination of orange and creamy yogurt creates a refreshing treat that's perfect for any time of day.

Kiwi Lime

Ingredients:

- 2 ripe kiwis, peeled and sliced
- Juice of 2 limes
- 1 banana
- 1 cup spinach leaves (optional, for added nutrients and color)
- 1 tablespoon honey or maple syrup (optional, for added sweetness)
- 1 cup water or coconut water
- Ice cubes (optional, for a colder smoothie)

Instructions:

1. Peel and slice the ripe kiwis.
2. Juice the limes to extract the fresh lime juice.
3. In a blender, combine the sliced kiwis, lime juice, banana, spinach leaves (if using), honey or maple syrup (if using), and water or coconut water.
4. Optionally, add a handful of ice cubes to the blender for a colder and more refreshing texture.
5. Blend all the ingredients together until smooth and creamy.
6. Taste the smoothie and adjust the sweetness by adding more honey or maple syrup if desired.
7. Once blended to your liking, pour the Kiwi Lime smoothie into glasses.
8. Optionally, garnish with a slice of kiwi or a wedge of lime on the rim of the glass.
9. Serve immediately and enjoy this zesty and nutritious Kiwi Lime smoothie! The combination of kiwi and lime creates a vibrant and energizing drink that's perfect for a quick and healthy snack.

Watermelon Mint

Ingredients:

- 2 cups fresh watermelon cubes (seedless)
- 5-6 fresh mint leaves
- Juice of 1 lime
- 1 tablespoon honey or agave syrup (optional, for added sweetness)
- 1/2 cup coconut water or water
- Ice cubes (optional, for a colder smoothie)

Instructions:

1. Cut the watermelon into cubes, ensuring they are seedless.
2. Wash the mint leaves thoroughly.
3. In a blender, combine the watermelon cubes, fresh mint leaves, lime juice, honey or agave syrup (if using), and coconut water or water.
4. Optionally, add a handful of ice cubes to the blender for a colder and more refreshing smoothie.
5. Blend all the ingredients together until smooth and well combined.
6. Taste the smoothie and adjust the sweetness by adding more honey or agave syrup if desired.
7. Once blended to your liking, pour the Watermelon Mint smoothie into glasses.
8. Optionally, garnish with a sprig of fresh mint on top for presentation.
9. Serve immediately and enjoy this hydrating and delicious Watermelon Mint smoothie! It's perfect for hot days and provides a burst of fruity freshness with a touch of minty coolness.

Cherry Vanilla

Ingredients:

- 1 cup frozen cherries (pitted)
- 1 ripe banana
- 1/2 cup Greek yogurt (plain or vanilla)
- 1/2 teaspoon vanilla extract
- 1 tablespoon honey or maple syrup (optional, for added sweetness)
- 1/2 cup almond milk (or any milk of your choice)
- Ice cubes (optional, for a colder smoothie)

Instructions:

1. Ensure the cherries are pitted before using them in the smoothie.
2. In a blender, combine the frozen cherries, ripe banana, Greek yogurt, vanilla extract, honey or maple syrup (if using), and almond milk.
3. If you prefer a thicker consistency, use less almond milk or add more frozen cherries.
4. Optionally, add a handful of ice cubes to the blender for a colder and thicker texture.
5. Blend all the ingredients together until smooth and creamy.
6. Taste the smoothie and adjust the sweetness by adding more honey or maple syrup if desired.
7. Once blended to your liking, pour the Cherry Vanilla smoothie into glasses.
8. Optionally, garnish with a few whole cherries on top for presentation.
9. Serve immediately and enjoy this delicious and fruity Cherry Vanilla smoothie! It's a perfect blend of sweet cherries with a hint of vanilla flavor, creating a delightful treat that's great for breakfast or a snack.

Spinach Berry

Ingredients:

- 1 cup fresh spinach leaves
- 1/2 cup frozen mixed berries (such as strawberries, blueberries, raspberries)
- 1 ripe banana
- 1/2 cup Greek yogurt (plain or vanilla)
- 1 tablespoon honey or maple syrup (optional, for added sweetness)
- 1 cup almond milk (or any milk of your choice)
- Ice cubes (optional, for a colder smoothie)

Instructions:

1. Wash the fresh spinach leaves thoroughly.
2. In a blender, combine the spinach leaves, frozen mixed berries, ripe banana, Greek yogurt, honey or maple syrup (if using), and almond milk.
3. Optionally, add a handful of ice cubes to the blender for a colder and more refreshing texture.
4. Blend all the ingredients together until smooth and creamy.
5. Taste the smoothie and adjust the sweetness by adding more honey or maple syrup if desired.
6. If the smoothie is too thick, add more almond milk gradually until you reach your desired consistency.
7. Once blended to your liking, pour the Spinach Berry smoothie into glasses.
8. Optionally, garnish with a few fresh berries on top for presentation.
9. Serve immediately and enjoy this nutritious and delicious Spinach Berry smoothie! It's a great way to incorporate leafy greens and berries into your diet in a tasty way.

Peanut Butter Banana

Ingredients:

- 1 ripe banana
- 2 tablespoons peanut butter (creamy or chunky)
- 1 cup milk (dairy or non-dairy, such as almond milk, soy milk, or oat milk)
- 1 tablespoon honey or maple syrup (optional, for added sweetness)
- Ice cubes (optional, for a colder smoothie)

Instructions:

1. Peel the ripe banana and break it into chunks.
2. In a blender, combine the banana chunks, peanut butter, milk, and honey or maple syrup (if using).
3. Optionally, add a handful of ice cubes to the blender for a colder and more refreshing smoothie.
4. Blend all the ingredients together until smooth and creamy.
5. Taste the smoothie and adjust the sweetness by adding more honey or maple syrup if desired.
6. If the smoothie is too thick, add more milk gradually until you reach your desired consistency.
7. Once blended to your liking, pour the Peanut Butter Banana smoothie into glasses.
8. Optionally, drizzle a little extra peanut butter on top for added flavor.
9. Serve immediately and enjoy this delicious and protein-rich Peanut Butter Banana smoothie! It's a great choice for breakfast or a post-workout snack to refuel and satisfy your cravings.

Turmeric Mango

Ingredients:

- 1 cup frozen mango chunks
- 1 ripe banana
- 1/2 teaspoon ground turmeric
- 1/2 teaspoon ground ginger (optional)
- 1 tablespoon honey or maple syrup (optional, for added sweetness)
- 1 cup coconut water or almond milk (or any milk of your choice)
- Ice cubes (optional, for a colder smoothie)

Instructions:

1. Ensure the mango chunks are frozen for a chilled smoothie.
2. Peel the ripe banana and break it into chunks.
3. In a blender, combine the frozen mango chunks, banana chunks, ground turmeric, ground ginger (if using), honey or maple syrup (if using), and coconut water or almond milk.
4. Optionally, add a handful of ice cubes to the blender for a colder and more refreshing smoothie.
5. Blend all the ingredients together until smooth and creamy.
6. Taste the smoothie and adjust the sweetness by adding more honey or maple syrup if desired.
7. If the smoothie is too thick, add more coconut water or almond milk gradually until you reach your desired consistency.
8. Once blended to your liking, pour the Turmeric Mango smoothie into glasses.
9. Serve immediately and enjoy this vibrant and immune-boosting smoothie! Turmeric adds a golden hue and anti-inflammatory properties, while mango provides sweetness and vitamin C.

Beetroot Berry

Ingredients:

- 1 small cooked beetroot (about 1/2 cup chopped)
- 1 cup mixed berries (such as strawberries, blueberries, raspberries)
- 1 ripe banana
- 1 cup spinach leaves (optional, for added nutrients)
- 1 tablespoon honey or maple syrup (optional, for added sweetness)
- 1 cup almond milk (or any milk of your choice)
- Ice cubes (optional, for a colder smoothie)

Instructions:

1. If using fresh beetroot, peel and chop it into small pieces. If using pre-cooked or canned beetroot, drain and rinse it.
2. In a blender, combine the cooked beetroot, mixed berries, ripe banana, spinach leaves (if using), honey or maple syrup (if using), and almond milk.
3. Optionally, add a handful of ice cubes to the blender for a colder and more refreshing smoothie.
4. Blend all the ingredients together until smooth and creamy.
5. Taste the smoothie and adjust the sweetness by adding more honey or maple syrup if desired.
6. If the smoothie is too thick, add more almond milk gradually until you reach your desired consistency.
7. Once blended to your liking, pour the Beetroot Berry smoothie into glasses.
8. Serve immediately and enjoy this vibrant and nutrient-packed smoothie! Beetroot adds a unique flavor and vibrant color, while mixed berries provide antioxidants and sweetness.

Cucumber Melon

Ingredients:

- 1 cup chopped cucumber (peeled and seeded)
- 1 cup chopped melon (such as honeydew or cantaloupe)
- 1/2 lime, juiced
- 1 tablespoon fresh mint leaves
- 1 tablespoon honey or agave syrup (optional, for added sweetness)
- 1 cup coconut water or water
- Ice cubes (optional, for a colder smoothie)

Instructions:

1. Peel and seed the cucumber, then chop it into chunks.
2. Chop the melon into cubes, removing seeds if necessary.
3. In a blender, combine the chopped cucumber, chopped melon, lime juice, fresh mint leaves, honey or agave syrup (if using), and coconut water or water.
4. Optionally, add a handful of ice cubes to the blender for a colder and more refreshing smoothie.
5. Blend all the ingredients together until smooth and well combined.
6. Taste the smoothie and adjust the sweetness by adding more honey or agave syrup if desired.
7. If the smoothie is too thick, add more coconut water or water gradually until you reach your desired consistency.
8. Once blended to your liking, pour the Cucumber Melon smoothie into glasses.
9. Optionally, garnish with a slice of cucumber or a sprig of mint on top for presentation.
10. Serve immediately and enjoy this cooling and revitalizing Cucumber Melon smoothie! It's perfect for hot days and provides a refreshing burst of flavors.

Mango Basil

Ingredients:

- 1 cup frozen mango chunks
- 1 ripe banana
- 5-6 fresh basil leaves
- 1 tablespoon honey or maple syrup (optional, for added sweetness)
- 1/2 cup plain Greek yogurt (or yogurt of your choice)
- 1/2 cup almond milk (or any milk of your choice)
- Ice cubes (optional, for a colder smoothie)

Instructions:

1. Ensure the mango chunks are frozen for a chilled smoothie.
2. In a blender, combine the frozen mango chunks, ripe banana, fresh basil leaves, honey or maple syrup (if using), Greek yogurt, and almond milk.
3. Optionally, add a handful of ice cubes to the blender for a colder and more refreshing smoothie.
4. Blend all the ingredients together until smooth and creamy.
5. Taste the smoothie and adjust the sweetness by adding more honey or maple syrup if desired.
6. If the smoothie is too thick, add more almond milk gradually until you reach your desired consistency.
7. Once blended to your liking, pour the Mango Basil smoothie into glasses.
8. Optionally, garnish with a fresh basil leaf on top for presentation.
9. Serve immediately and enjoy this unique and flavorful Mango Basil smoothie! The combination of mango and basil creates a delightful tropical taste with an herbal twist.

Strawberry Kiwi

Ingredients:

- 1 cup fresh strawberries, hulled and halved
- 2 ripe kiwis, peeled and sliced
- 1 banana
- 1/2 cup plain Greek yogurt (or yogurt of your choice)
- 1 tablespoon honey or maple syrup (optional, for added sweetness)
- 1/2 cup almond milk (or any milk of your choice)
- Ice cubes (optional, for a colder smoothie)

Instructions:

1. Prepare the strawberries by removing the stems and slicing them in half.
2. Peel the kiwis and slice them into smaller pieces.
3. Peel the banana and break it into chunks.
4. In a blender, combine the strawberries, kiwi slices, banana chunks, Greek yogurt, honey or maple syrup (if using), and almond milk.
5. Optionally, add a handful of ice cubes to the blender for a colder and more refreshing smoothie.
6. Blend all the ingredients together until smooth and creamy.
7. Taste the smoothie and adjust the sweetness by adding more honey or maple syrup if desired.
8. If the smoothie is too thick, add more almond milk gradually until you reach your desired consistency.
9. Once blended to your liking, pour the Strawberry Kiwi smoothie into glasses.
10. Optionally, garnish with a slice of kiwi or a strawberry on the rim of the glass for presentation.
11. Serve immediately and enjoy this delightful Strawberry Kiwi smoothie! It's a perfect blend of sweet strawberries and tangy kiwi that's great for breakfast or a refreshing snack.

Apple Pie (Apple, Cinnamon, Oats)

Ingredients:

- 1 medium apple, cored and chopped (peeled or unpeeled, based on preference)
- 1/2 cup rolled oats
- 1/2 teaspoon ground cinnamon
- 1 tablespoon honey or maple syrup (optional, for added sweetness)
- 1 cup milk (dairy or non-dairy, such as almond milk or oat milk)
- Ice cubes (optional, for a colder smoothie)

Instructions:

1. Prepare the apple by coring and chopping it into chunks.
2. In a blender, combine the chopped apple, rolled oats, ground cinnamon, honey or maple syrup (if using), and milk.
3. Optionally, add a handful of ice cubes to the blender for a colder smoothie.
4. Blend all the ingredients together until smooth and creamy.
5. Taste the smoothie and adjust the sweetness by adding more honey or maple syrup if desired.
6. If the smoothie is too thick, add more milk gradually until you reach your desired consistency.
7. Once blended to your liking, pour the Apple Pie smoothie into glasses.
8. Optionally, sprinkle a little extra cinnamon on top for garnish.
9. Serve immediately and enjoy this nutritious and comforting Apple Pie smoothie! It's a delightful way to enjoy the flavors of apple pie in a healthy and satisfying drink.

Pineapple Ginger

Ingredients:

- 1 cup frozen pineapple chunks
- 1-inch piece of fresh ginger, peeled and grated (adjust amount to taste)
- 1 ripe banana
- 1/2 cup plain Greek yogurt (or yogurt of your choice)
- 1 tablespoon honey or maple syrup (optional, for added sweetness)
- 1/2 cup coconut water or water
- Ice cubes (optional, for a colder smoothie)

Instructions:

1. Peel and grate the fresh ginger to get about 1 tablespoon of grated ginger.
2. In a blender, combine the frozen pineapple chunks, grated ginger, ripe banana, Greek yogurt, honey or maple syrup (if using), and coconut water or water.
3. Optionally, add a handful of ice cubes to the blender for a colder and more refreshing smoothie.
4. Blend all the ingredients together until smooth and creamy.
5. Taste the smoothie and adjust the sweetness by adding more honey or maple syrup if desired.
6. If the smoothie is too thick, add more coconut water or water gradually until you reach your desired consistency.
7. Once blended to your liking, pour the Pineapple Ginger smoothie into glasses.
8. Optionally, garnish with a slice of pineapple or a sprinkle of grated ginger on top for presentation.
9. Serve immediately and enjoy this invigorating and tropical Pineapple Ginger smoothie! The combination of sweet pineapple and spicy ginger creates a wonderful flavor that's perfect for a refreshing treat.

Carrot Cake Smoothie

Ingredients:

- 1 medium carrot, peeled and chopped
- 1 ripe banana
- 1/2 cup rolled oats
- 1/2 teaspoon ground cinnamon
- 1/4 teaspoon ground nutmeg
- 1 tablespoon honey or maple syrup (optional, for added sweetness)
- 1 cup almond milk (or any milk of your choice)
- 1/4 cup plain Greek yogurt (or yogurt of your choice)
- 1/4 cup crushed pineapple (canned or fresh)
- Ice cubes (optional, for a colder smoothie)
- Chopped walnuts or pecans for garnish (optional)

Instructions:

1. Peel and chop the carrot into smaller pieces.
2. In a blender, combine the chopped carrot, ripe banana, rolled oats, ground cinnamon, ground nutmeg, honey or maple syrup (if using), almond milk, Greek yogurt, and crushed pineapple.
3. Optionally, add a handful of ice cubes to the blender for a colder and more refreshing smoothie.
4. Blend all the ingredients together until smooth and creamy.
5. Taste the smoothie and adjust the sweetness or spice level by adding more honey, cinnamon, or nutmeg if desired.
6. If the smoothie is too thick, add more almond milk gradually until you reach your desired consistency.
7. Once blended to your liking, pour the Carrot Cake Smoothie into glasses.
8. Optionally, garnish with chopped walnuts or pecans on top for added texture and flavor.
9. Serve immediately and enjoy this nutritious and satisfying Carrot Cake Smoothie! It's a wholesome way to enjoy the flavors of carrot cake in a convenient and delicious drink.

Mixed Citrus (Orange, Grapefruit, Lemon)

Ingredients:

- 1 orange, peeled and segmented
- 1/2 grapefruit, peeled and segmented
- Juice of 1 lemon
- 1 ripe banana
- 1 tablespoon honey or maple syrup (optional, for added sweetness)
- 1/2 cup Greek yogurt (plain or vanilla)
- 1/2 cup water or coconut water
- Ice cubes (optional, for a colder smoothie)

Instructions:

1. Peel and segment the orange and grapefruit, removing any seeds.
2. Juice the lemon to extract fresh lemon juice.
3. In a blender, combine the orange segments, grapefruit segments, lemon juice, ripe banana, honey or maple syrup (if using), Greek yogurt, and water or coconut water.
4. Optionally, add a handful of ice cubes to the blender for a colder and more refreshing smoothie.
5. Blend all the ingredients together until smooth and well combined.
6. Taste the smoothie and adjust the sweetness by adding more honey or maple syrup if desired.
7. If the smoothie is too thick, add more water or coconut water gradually until you reach your desired consistency.
8. Once blended to your liking, pour the Mixed Citrus smoothie into glasses.
9. Serve immediately and enjoy this tangy and invigorating citrus smoothie! It's a wonderful way to start your day with a burst of vitamin C and refreshing citrus flavors.

Raspberry Lemonade

Ingredients:

- 1 cup frozen raspberries
- Juice of 2-3 lemons (about 1/2 cup of lemon juice)
- 1 tablespoon honey or maple syrup (adjust to taste)
- 1/2 cup Greek yogurt (plain or vanilla)
- 1/2 cup water
- Ice cubes (optional, for a colder smoothie)

Instructions:

1. In a blender, combine the frozen raspberries, freshly squeezed lemon juice, honey or maple syrup, Greek yogurt, and water.
2. Optionally, add a handful of ice cubes to the blender for a colder and more refreshing smoothie.
3. Blend all the ingredients together until smooth and creamy.
4. Taste the smoothie and adjust the sweetness by adding more honey or maple syrup if desired.
5. If the smoothie is too thick, add more water gradually until you reach your desired consistency.
6. Once blended to your liking, pour the Raspberry Lemonade smoothie into glasses.
7. Optionally, garnish with a slice of lemon or a few whole raspberries on top for presentation.
8. Serve immediately and enjoy this delightful and tangy Raspberry Lemonade smoothie! It's perfect for a sunny day or any time you're craving a refreshing drink with a twist of raspberry and lemon flavors.

Chocolate Cherry

Ingredients:

- 1 cup frozen cherries (pitted)
- 1 tablespoon cocoa powder (unsweetened)
- 1 ripe banana
- 1 tablespoon almond butter (or peanut butter)
- 1 cup almond milk (or any milk of your choice)
- 1 tablespoon honey or maple syrup (optional, for added sweetness)
- Ice cubes (optional, for a colder smoothie)

Instructions:

1. Place the frozen cherries, cocoa powder, ripe banana, almond butter, almond milk, and honey or maple syrup (if using) in a blender.
2. Optionally, add a handful of ice cubes to the blender for a colder and thicker smoothie.
3. Blend all the ingredients together until smooth and creamy.
4. Taste the smoothie and adjust the sweetness by adding more honey or maple syrup if desired.
5. If the smoothie is too thick, add more almond milk gradually until you reach your desired consistency.
6. Once blended to your liking, pour the Chocolate Cherry smoothie into glasses.
7. Serve immediately and enjoy this delightful and indulgent smoothie! The combination of chocolate and cherries creates a heavenly flavor that's perfect for a satisfying treat or dessert.

Avocado Matcha

Ingredients:

- 1 ripe avocado, peeled and pitted
- 1 teaspoon matcha green tea powder
- 1 tablespoon honey or maple syrup (optional, for added sweetness)
- 1 banana
- 1 cup almond milk (or any milk of your choice)
- Ice cubes (optional, for a colder smoothie)

Instructions:

1. In a blender, combine the ripe avocado, matcha green tea powder, honey or maple syrup (if using), banana, and almond milk.
2. Optionally, add a handful of ice cubes to the blender for a colder and more refreshing smoothie.
3. Blend all the ingredients together until smooth and creamy.
4. Taste the smoothie and adjust the sweetness by adding more honey or maple syrup if desired.
5. If the smoothie is too thick, add more almond milk gradually until you reach your desired consistency.
6. Once blended to your liking, pour the Avocado Matcha smoothie into glasses.
7. Optionally, sprinkle a little extra matcha powder on top for garnish.
8. Serve immediately and enjoy this nutritious and delicious Avocado Matcha smoothie! It's a great way to incorporate the benefits of avocado and matcha into a tasty and energizing drink.

Blueberry Lavender

Ingredients:

- 1 cup frozen blueberries
- 1 ripe banana
- 1 tablespoon dried culinary lavender buds (or 1-2 drops of food-grade lavender essential oil)
- 1 tablespoon honey or maple syrup (optional, for added sweetness)
- 1 cup almond milk (or any milk of your choice)
- Ice cubes (optional, for a colder smoothie)

Instructions:

1. In a blender, combine the frozen blueberries, ripe banana, dried culinary lavender buds (or lavender essential oil), honey or maple syrup (if using), and almond milk.
2. Optionally, add a handful of ice cubes to the blender for a colder and more refreshing smoothie.
3. Blend all the ingredients together until smooth and creamy.
4. Taste the smoothie and adjust the sweetness by adding more honey or maple syrup if desired.
5. If using dried lavender buds, you may strain the smoothie through a fine mesh sieve to remove any lavender pieces before serving.
6. Once blended to your liking, pour the Blueberry Lavender smoothie into glasses.
7. Optionally, garnish with a few fresh blueberries or a sprinkle of dried lavender buds on top for presentation.
8. Serve immediately and enjoy this unique and soothing Blueberry Lavender smoothie! It's a lovely combination of flavors that's both delicious and relaxing.

Cranberry Orange

Ingredients:

- 1 cup fresh or frozen cranberries
- Juice of 2 oranges
- 1 ripe banana
- 1 tablespoon honey or maple syrup (optional, for added sweetness)
- 1/2 cup Greek yogurt (plain or vanilla)
- 1/2 cup water or orange juice (for blending)

Instructions:

1. If using fresh cranberries, rinse them thoroughly. If using frozen cranberries, thaw them slightly.
2. Juice the oranges to extract fresh orange juice.
3. In a blender, combine the cranberries, orange juice, ripe banana, honey or maple syrup (if using), Greek yogurt, and water or additional orange juice.
4. Blend all the ingredients together until smooth and creamy.
5. Taste the smoothie and adjust the sweetness by adding more honey or maple syrup if desired.
6. If the smoothie is too thick, add more water or orange juice gradually until you reach your desired consistency.
7. Once blended to your liking, pour the Cranberry Orange smoothie into glasses.
8. Optionally, garnish with a slice of orange or a few whole cranberries on top for presentation.
9. Serve immediately and enjoy this vibrant and tangy Cranberry Orange smoothie! It's perfect for a refreshing breakfast or a healthy snack packed with vitamin C and antioxidants.

Banana Chai

Ingredients:

- 1 ripe banana
- 1 cup brewed chai tea, cooled (use your favorite chai tea blend)
- 1/2 cup plain Greek yogurt (or yogurt of your choice)
- 1 tablespoon honey or maple syrup (optional, for added sweetness)
- 1/2 teaspoon ground cinnamon
- 1/4 teaspoon ground ginger
- 1/4 teaspoon ground cardamom
- Pinch of ground cloves
- Pinch of ground nutmeg
- Ice cubes (optional, for a colder smoothie)

Instructions:

1. Brew a cup of chai tea using your preferred chai tea blend and allow it to cool to room temperature.
2. In a blender, combine the ripe banana, cooled chai tea, Greek yogurt, honey or maple syrup (if using), and all the ground spices (cinnamon, ginger, cardamom, cloves, nutmeg).
3. Optionally, add a handful of ice cubes to the blender for a colder and more refreshing smoothie.
4. Blend all the ingredients together until smooth and creamy.
5. Taste the smoothie and adjust the sweetness by adding more honey or maple syrup if desired.
6. If the smoothie is too thick, add a little more brewed chai tea or water gradually until you reach your desired consistency.
7. Once blended to your liking, pour the Banana Chai smoothie into glasses.
8. Optionally, sprinkle a little extra ground cinnamon on top for garnish.
9. Serve immediately and enjoy this aromatic and spiced Banana Chai smoothie! It's a delightful twist on a classic chai tea flavor combined with the creaminess of banana and yogurt.

Spinach Mango

Ingredients:

- 1 cup fresh spinach leaves
- 1 ripe mango, peeled and diced (or 1 cup frozen mango chunks)
- 1 banana
- 1 tablespoon chia seeds or flax seeds (optional)
- 1 cup almond milk (or any milk of your choice)
- Ice cubes (optional, for a colder smoothie)
- Honey or maple syrup (optional, for added sweetness)

Instructions:

1. Wash the fresh spinach leaves thoroughly.
2. Peel and dice the ripe mango, or use pre-cut frozen mango chunks.
3. In a blender, combine the spinach leaves, diced mango (or frozen mango chunks), banana, chia seeds or flax seeds (if using), and almond milk.
4. Optionally, add a handful of ice cubes to the blender for a colder and more refreshing smoothie.
5. Blend all the ingredients together until smooth and creamy.
6. Taste the smoothie and add honey or maple syrup if you prefer a sweeter taste.
7. If the smoothie is too thick, add more almond milk gradually until you reach your desired consistency.
8. Once blended to your liking, pour the Spinach Mango smoothie into glasses.
9. Serve immediately and enjoy this vibrant and nutrient-packed smoothie! It's a great way to incorporate spinach and mango into a delicious and healthy drink.

Honeydew Lime

Ingredients:

- 2 cups diced honeydew melon
- Juice of 2 limes
- 1 banana
- 1 tablespoon honey or agave syrup (optional, for added sweetness)
- 1/2 cup Greek yogurt (plain or vanilla)
- 1/2 cup coconut water or water
- Ice cubes (optional, for a colder smoothie)

Instructions:

1. Dice the honeydew melon to get about 2 cups of diced melon.
2. Juice the limes to extract fresh lime juice.
3. In a blender, combine the diced honeydew melon, lime juice, banana, honey or agave syrup (if using), Greek yogurt, and coconut water or water.
4. Optionally, add a handful of ice cubes to the blender for a colder and more refreshing smoothie.
5. Blend all the ingredients together until smooth and creamy.
6. Taste the smoothie and adjust the sweetness by adding more honey or agave syrup if desired.
7. If the smoothie is too thick, add more coconut water or water gradually until you reach your desired consistency.
8. Once blended to your liking, pour the Honeydew Lime smoothie into glasses.
9. Serve immediately and enjoy this delightful and hydrating smoothie! The combination of honeydew and lime creates a tropical and tangy flavor that's perfect for a refreshing drink.

Berry Beet

Ingredients:

- 1 small cooked beetroot (about 1/2 cup chopped)
- 1 cup mixed berries (such as strawberries, blueberries, raspberries)
- 1 ripe banana
- 1 tablespoon chia seeds or flax seeds (optional)
- 1 cup almond milk (or any milk of your choice)
- Ice cubes (optional, for a colder smoothie)
- Honey or maple syrup (optional, for added sweetness)

Instructions:

1. Prepare the cooked beetroot by peeling and chopping it into chunks.
2. In a blender, combine the chopped beetroot, mixed berries, ripe banana, chia seeds or flax seeds (if using), and almond milk.
3. Optionally, add a handful of ice cubes to the blender for a colder and more refreshing smoothie.
4. Blend all the ingredients together until smooth and creamy.
5. Taste the smoothie and add honey or maple syrup if you prefer a sweeter taste.
6. If the smoothie is too thick, add more almond milk gradually until you reach your desired consistency.
7. Once blended to your liking, pour the Berry Beet smoothie into glasses.
8. Optionally, garnish with fresh berries or a sprinkle of chia seeds on top for presentation.
9. Serve immediately and enjoy this nutrient-packed and colorful smoothie! The combination of berries and beets provides antioxidants, vitamins, and natural sweetness.

Mango Turmeric

Ingredients:

- 1 ripe mango, peeled and diced
- 1 banana
- 1 teaspoon ground turmeric
- 1/2 teaspoon ground ginger
- Juice of 1 lemon
- 1 tablespoon honey or maple syrup (optional, for added sweetness)
- 1 cup coconut water or water
- Ice cubes (optional, for a colder smoothie)

Instructions:

1. Peel and dice the ripe mango.
2. In a blender, combine the diced mango, banana, ground turmeric, ground ginger, lemon juice, honey or maple syrup (if using), and coconut water or water.
3. Optionally, add a handful of ice cubes to the blender for a colder and more refreshing smoothie.
4. Blend all the ingredients together until smooth and creamy.
5. Taste the smoothie and adjust the sweetness by adding more honey or maple syrup if desired.
6. If the smoothie is too thick, add more coconut water or water gradually until you reach your desired consistency.
7. Once blended to your liking, pour the Mango Turmeric smoothie into glasses.
8. Serve immediately and enjoy this vibrant and immune-boosting smoothie! The combination of mango and turmeric provides a burst of tropical flavor along with anti-inflammatory properties from the turmeric.

Vanilla Fig

Ingredients:

- 4-5 ripe figs, stemmed and quartered
- 1 ripe banana
- 1 cup Greek yogurt (plain or vanilla)
- 1 teaspoon vanilla extract
- 1 tablespoon honey or maple syrup (optional, for added sweetness)
- 1/2 cup almond milk (or any milk of your choice)
- Ice cubes (optional, for a colder smoothie)

Instructions:

1. Prepare the ripe figs by removing the stems and quartering them.
2. In a blender, combine the quartered figs, banana, Greek yogurt, vanilla extract, honey or maple syrup (if using), and almond milk.
3. Optionally, add a handful of ice cubes to the blender for a colder and thicker smoothie.
4. Blend all the ingredients together until smooth and creamy.
5. Taste the smoothie and adjust the sweetness by adding more honey or maple syrup if desired.
6. If the smoothie is too thick, add more almond milk gradually until you reach your desired consistency.
7. Once blended to your liking, pour the Vanilla Fig smoothie into glasses.
8. Optionally, garnish with a slice of fresh fig or a sprinkle of cinnamon on top for presentation.
9. Serve immediately and enjoy this delicious and unique Vanilla Fig smoothie! It's a wonderful way to enjoy the natural sweetness and richness of figs combined with creamy vanilla flavors.

Strawberry Rhubarb

Ingredients:

- 1 cup chopped rhubarb (fresh or frozen)
- 1 cup fresh strawberries, hulled and halved
- 1 ripe banana
- 1 tablespoon honey or maple syrup (optional, for added sweetness)
- 1 cup Greek yogurt (plain or vanilla)
- 1/2 cup almond milk (or any milk of your choice)
- Ice cubes (optional, for a colder smoothie)

Instructions:

1. If using fresh rhubarb, chop it into small pieces.
2. In a saucepan, cook the chopped rhubarb with a little water over medium heat until it becomes soft and starts to break down. Let it cool slightly.
3. In a blender, combine the cooked rhubarb, fresh strawberries, ripe banana, honey or maple syrup (if using), Greek yogurt, and almond milk.
4. Optionally, add a handful of ice cubes to the blender for a colder and more refreshing smoothie.
5. Blend all the ingredients together until smooth and creamy.
6. Taste the smoothie and adjust the sweetness by adding more honey or maple syrup if desired.
7. If the smoothie is too thick, add more almond milk gradually until you reach your desired consistency.
8. Once blended to your liking, pour the Strawberry Rhubarb smoothie into glasses.
9. Serve immediately and enjoy this delightful and tangy smoothie! It's a perfect way to savor the flavors of strawberry and rhubarb in a healthy and satisfying drink.

Pumpkin Spice

Ingredients:

- 1/2 cup pumpkin puree (canned or homemade)
- 1 ripe banana
- 1/2 cup Greek yogurt (plain or vanilla)
- 1 tablespoon maple syrup or honey (adjust to taste)
- 1/2 teaspoon pumpkin pie spice (or a blend of cinnamon, nutmeg, ginger, and cloves)
- 1 cup almond milk (or any milk of your choice)
- Ice cubes (optional, for a colder smoothie)

Instructions:

1. In a blender, combine the pumpkin puree, ripe banana, Greek yogurt, maple syrup or honey, pumpkin pie spice, and almond milk.
2. Optionally, add a handful of ice cubes to the blender for a colder and thicker smoothie.
3. Blend all the ingredients together until smooth and creamy.
4. Taste the smoothie and adjust the sweetness or spice level by adding more maple syrup, honey, or pumpkin pie spice if desired.
5. If the smoothie is too thick, add more almond milk gradually until you reach your desired consistency.
6. Once blended to your liking, pour the Pumpkin Spice smoothie into glasses.
7. Optionally, sprinkle a little extra pumpkin pie spice on top for garnish.
8. Serve immediately and enjoy this cozy and flavorful smoothie! It's a delightful way to indulge in the taste of pumpkin spice, perfect for autumn or any time you're craving a taste of fall.

Pineapple Jalapeño

Ingredients:

- 1 cup frozen pineapple chunks
- 1 small jalapeño pepper, seeds removed and chopped
- 1 banana
- Juice of 1 lime
- 1 tablespoon honey or agave syrup (optional, for added sweetness)
- 1 cup coconut water or water
- Ice cubes (optional, for a colder smoothie)

Instructions:

1. Prepare the ingredients by cutting and measuring the pineapple chunks, chopping the jalapeño pepper (remove seeds for less heat), and peeling the banana.
2. In a blender, combine the frozen pineapple chunks, chopped jalapeño pepper, banana, lime juice, honey or agave syrup (if using), and coconut water or water.
3. Optionally, add a handful of ice cubes to the blender for a colder and more refreshing smoothie.
4. Blend all the ingredients together until smooth and well combined.
5. Taste the smoothie and adjust the sweetness or spice level by adding more honey/agave or jalapeño, depending on your preference.
6. If the smoothie is too thick, add more coconut water or water gradually until you reach your desired consistency.
7. Once blended to your liking, pour the Pineapple Jalapeño smoothie into glasses.
8. Optionally, garnish with a slice of jalapeño or a wedge of lime on the rim of the glass for presentation.
9. Serve immediately and enjoy this exciting and flavorful smoothie! The sweet pineapple complements the spicy kick of jalapeño for a refreshing and adventurous drink. Adjust the spice level to suit your taste buds!

Coconut Lime

Ingredients:

- 1 cup coconut milk (canned, full-fat for creaminess)
- Juice and zest of 2 limes
- 1 tablespoon honey or agave syrup (optional, for added sweetness)
- 1 frozen banana
- 1/2 cup frozen pineapple chunks
- Ice cubes (optional, for a colder smoothie)
- Unsweetened shredded coconut for garnish (optional)

Instructions:

1. In a blender, combine the coconut milk, lime juice, lime zest, honey or agave syrup (if using), frozen banana, and frozen pineapple chunks.
2. Optionally, add a handful of ice cubes to the blender for a colder and more refreshing smoothie.
3. Blend all the ingredients together until smooth and creamy.
4. Taste the smoothie and adjust the sweetness by adding more honey or agave syrup if desired.
5. If the smoothie is too thick, add more coconut milk or a splash of water gradually until you reach your desired consistency.
6. Once blended to your liking, pour the Coconut Lime smoothie into glasses.
7. Optionally, sprinkle some unsweetened shredded coconut on top for garnish.
8. Serve immediately and enjoy this tropical and tangy Coconut Lime smoothie! It's a delightful combination of creamy coconut and zesty lime that will transport you to a sunny paradise.

Chocolate Raspberry

Ingredients:

- 1 cup frozen raspberries
- 2 tablespoons cocoa powder (unsweetened)
- 1 ripe banana
- 1 tablespoon honey or maple syrup (optional, for added sweetness)
- 1 cup almond milk (or any milk of your choice)
- Ice cubes (optional, for a colder smoothie)

Instructions:

1. In a blender, combine the frozen raspberries, cocoa powder, ripe banana, honey or maple syrup (if using), and almond milk.
2. Optionally, add a handful of ice cubes to the blender for a colder and thicker smoothie.
3. Blend all the ingredients together until smooth and creamy.
4. Taste the smoothie and adjust the sweetness by adding more honey or maple syrup if desired.
5. If the smoothie is too thick, add more almond milk gradually until you reach your desired consistency.
6. Once blended to your liking, pour the Chocolate Raspberry smoothie into glasses.
7. Optionally, garnish with a few fresh raspberries on top for presentation.
8. Serve immediately and enjoy this delightful and indulgent smoothie! The combination of chocolate and raspberries creates a heavenly flavor that's perfect for a satisfying treat or dessert.

Almond Date

Ingredients:

- 5-6 pitted dates
- 1 banana
- 2 tablespoons almond butter or 1/4 cup raw almonds
- 1 cup almond milk (or any milk of your choice)
- 1/2 teaspoon vanilla extract
- Ice cubes (optional, for a colder smoothie)

Instructions:

1. Soak the pitted dates in warm water for about 10-15 minutes to soften them.
2. In a blender, combine the soaked dates (drained), banana, almond butter (or raw almonds), almond milk, and vanilla extract.
3. Optionally, add a handful of ice cubes to the blender for a colder and thicker smoothie.
4. Blend all the ingredients together until smooth and creamy.
5. Taste the smoothie and adjust the sweetness by adding more dates or a touch of honey or maple syrup if desired.
6. If the smoothie is too thick, add more almond milk gradually until you reach your desired consistency.
7. Once blended to your liking, pour the Almond Date smoothie into glasses.
8. Optionally, garnish with a sprinkle of ground cinnamon or chopped almonds on top for presentation.
9. Serve immediately and enjoy this delicious and satisfying Almond Date smoothie! It's a great way to enjoy the natural sweetness of dates along with the nutty flavor of almonds in a nutritious drink.

Green Tea Pear

Ingredients:

- 1 ripe pear, cored and chopped
- 1 teaspoon matcha green tea powder
- 1 banana
- 1 tablespoon honey or maple syrup (optional, for added sweetness)
- 1 cup almond milk (or any milk of your choice)
- Ice cubes (optional, for a colder smoothie)

Instructions:

1. Prepare the ripe pear by coring and chopping it into chunks.
2. In a blender, combine the chopped pear, matcha green tea powder, banana, honey or maple syrup (if using), and almond milk.
3. Optionally, add a handful of ice cubes to the blender for a colder and more refreshing smoothie.
4. Blend all the ingredients together until smooth and creamy.
5. Taste the smoothie and adjust the sweetness by adding more honey or maple syrup if desired.
6. If the smoothie is too thick, add more almond milk gradually until you reach your desired consistency.
7. Once blended to your liking, pour the Green Tea Pear smoothie into glasses.
8. Serve immediately and enjoy this delightful and energizing smoothie! The combination of green tea and pear provides antioxidants, vitamins, and a refreshing taste.

Plum Ginger

Ingredients:

- 2 ripe plums, pitted and chopped
- 1-inch piece of fresh ginger, peeled and grated
- 1 banana
- 1 tablespoon honey or maple syrup (optional, for added sweetness)
- 1 cup almond milk (or any milk of your choice)
- Ice cubes (optional, for a colder smoothie)

Instructions:

1. Prepare the ripe plums by removing the pits and chopping them into chunks.
2. Peel and grate the fresh ginger to get about 1 tablespoon of grated ginger.
3. In a blender, combine the chopped plums, grated ginger, banana, honey or maple syrup (if using), and almond milk.
4. Optionally, add a handful of ice cubes to the blender for a colder and more refreshing smoothie.
5. Blend all the ingredients together until smooth and creamy.
6. Taste the smoothie and adjust the sweetness by adding more honey or maple syrup if desired.
7. If the smoothie is too thick, add more almond milk gradually until you reach your desired consistency.
8. Once blended to your liking, pour the Plum Ginger smoothie into glasses.
9. Serve immediately and enjoy this unique and flavorful smoothie! The combination of sweet plums with zesty ginger creates a delicious and invigorating drink.

Blackberry Basil

Ingredients:

- 1 cup fresh blackberries (or frozen)
- 5-6 fresh basil leaves
- 1 banana
- 1 tablespoon honey or maple syrup (optional, for added sweetness)
- Juice of 1 lime
- 1 cup almond milk (or any milk of your choice)
- Ice cubes (optional, for a colder smoothie)

Instructions:

1. Rinse the fresh blackberries and basil leaves under cold water.
2. In a blender, combine the blackberries, basil leaves, banana, honey or maple syrup (if using), lime juice, and almond milk.
3. Optionally, add a handful of ice cubes to the blender for a colder and more refreshing smoothie.
4. Blend all the ingredients together until smooth and creamy.
5. Taste the smoothie and adjust the sweetness by adding more honey or maple syrup if desired.
6. If the smoothie is too thick, add more almond milk gradually until you reach your desired consistency.
7. Once blended to your liking, pour the Blackberry Basil smoothie into glasses.
8. Optionally, garnish with a fresh basil leaf or a few whole blackberries on top for presentation.
9. Serve immediately and enjoy this delightful and unique smoothie! The combination of blackberries and basil creates a delicious blend of sweet and herbal flavors that's perfect for a refreshing drink.

Strawberry Shortcake

Ingredients:

- 1 cup fresh strawberries, hulled and halved
- 1 banana
- 1/2 cup Greek yogurt (plain or vanilla)
- 1/2 cup rolled oats
- 1 tablespoon honey or maple syrup (optional, for added sweetness)
- 1 teaspoon vanilla extract
- 1 cup almond milk (or any milk of your choice)
- Ice cubes (optional, for a colder smoothie)

Instructions:

1. In a blender, combine the fresh strawberries, banana, Greek yogurt, rolled oats, honey or maple syrup (if using), vanilla extract, and almond milk.
2. Optionally, add a handful of ice cubes to the blender for a colder and thicker smoothie.
3. Blend all the ingredients together until smooth and creamy.
4. Taste the smoothie and adjust the sweetness by adding more honey or maple syrup if desired.
5. If the smoothie is too thick, add more almond milk gradually until you reach your desired consistency.
6. Once blended to your liking, pour the Strawberry Shortcake smoothie into glasses.
7. Optionally, garnish with a strawberry slice or a sprinkle of oats on top for presentation.
8. Serve immediately and enjoy this delicious and satisfying smoothie that tastes like strawberry shortcake in a glass! The addition of oats provides a cake-like texture and adds a touch of heartiness to the drink.

Peach Raspberry

Ingredients:

- 1 cup fresh or frozen peaches, sliced
- 1 cup fresh or frozen raspberries
- 1 banana
- 1/2 cup Greek yogurt (plain or vanilla)
- 1 tablespoon honey or maple syrup (optional, for added sweetness)
- 1 cup almond milk (or any milk of your choice)
- Ice cubes (optional, for a colder smoothie)

Instructions:

1. In a blender, combine the sliced peaches, raspberries, banana, Greek yogurt, honey or maple syrup (if using), and almond milk.
2. Optionally, add a handful of ice cubes to the blender for a colder and thicker smoothie.
3. Blend all the ingredients together until smooth and creamy.
4. Taste the smoothie and adjust the sweetness by adding more honey or maple syrup if desired.
5. If the smoothie is too thick, add more almond milk gradually until you reach your desired consistency.
6. Once blended to your liking, pour the Peach Raspberry smoothie into glasses.
7. Optionally, garnish with a fresh raspberry or peach slice on the rim of the glass for presentation.
8. Serve immediately and enjoy this delightful and fruity smoothie! The combination of peach and raspberry creates a burst of flavors that's perfect for a refreshing and healthy drink.

Blueberry Cardamom

Ingredients:

- 1 cup fresh or frozen blueberries
- 1 banana
- 1/2 teaspoon ground cardamom
- 1 tablespoon honey or maple syrup (optional, for added sweetness)
- 1 cup Greek yogurt (plain or vanilla)
- 1 cup almond milk (or any milk of your choice)
- Ice cubes (optional, for a colder smoothie)

Instructions:

1. In a blender, combine the blueberries, banana, ground cardamom, honey or maple syrup (if using), Greek yogurt, and almond milk.
2. Optionally, add a handful of ice cubes to the blender for a colder and thicker smoothie.
3. Blend all the ingredients together until smooth and creamy.
4. Taste the smoothie and adjust the sweetness by adding more honey or maple syrup if desired.
5. If the smoothie is too thick, add more almond milk gradually until you reach your desired consistency.
6. Once blended to your liking, pour the Blueberry Cardamom smoothie into glasses.
7. Optionally, sprinkle a pinch of ground cardamom on top for garnish.
8. Serve immediately and enjoy this delicious and aromatic smoothie! The combination of blueberries with the warm spice of cardamom creates a unique and delightful flavor experience.

Mango Mint

Ingredients:

- 1 ripe mango, peeled and diced
- 1 banana
- 1 tablespoon fresh mint leaves (about 8-10 leaves)
- Juice of 1 lime
- 1 tablespoon honey or maple syrup (optional, for added sweetness)
- 1 cup coconut water or water
- Ice cubes (optional, for a colder smoothie)

Instructions:

1. Peel and dice the ripe mango.
2. In a blender, combine the diced mango, banana, fresh mint leaves, lime juice, honey or maple syrup (if using), and coconut water or water.
3. Optionally, add a handful of ice cubes to the blender for a colder and more refreshing smoothie.
4. Blend all the ingredients together until smooth and creamy.
5. Taste the smoothie and adjust the sweetness by adding more honey or maple syrup if desired.
6. If the smoothie is too thick, add more coconut water or water gradually until you reach your desired consistency.
7. Once blended to your liking, pour the Mango Mint smoothie into glasses.
8. Optionally, garnish with a sprig of fresh mint or a slice of lime on the rim of the glass for presentation.
9. Serve immediately and enjoy this delightful and tropical smoothie! The combination of mango and mint creates a refreshing and invigorating drink that's perfect for a sunny day.

Cherry Almond

Ingredients:

- 1 cup fresh or frozen cherries, pitted
- 1 banana
- 1 tablespoon almond butter
- 1 cup almond milk (or any milk of your choice)
- 1 tablespoon honey or maple syrup (optional, for added sweetness)
- Ice cubes (optional, for a colder smoothie)

Instructions:

1. If using fresh cherries, remove the pits. If using frozen cherries, thaw them slightly.
2. In a blender, combine the cherries, banana, almond butter, almond milk, and honey or maple syrup (if using).
3. Optionally, add a handful of ice cubes to the blender for a colder and thicker smoothie.
4. Blend all the ingredients together until smooth and creamy.
5. Taste the smoothie and adjust the sweetness by adding more honey or maple syrup if desired.
6. If the smoothie is too thick, add more almond milk gradually until you reach your desired consistency.
7. Once blended to your liking, pour the Cherry Almond smoothie into glasses.
8. Optionally, garnish with a few whole cherries or a sprinkle of sliced almonds on top for presentation.
9. Serve immediately and enjoy this delicious and satisfying Cherry Almond smoothie! The combination of cherries and almond butter provides a delightful flavor with a hint of nuttiness that's perfect for a nutritious drink.

Raspberry Hibiscus

Ingredients:

- 1 cup fresh or frozen raspberries
- 1 tablespoon dried hibiscus flowers (or hibiscus tea)
- 1 banana
- 1 tablespoon honey or agave syrup (optional, for added sweetness)
- 1 cup coconut water or water
- Ice cubes (optional, for a colder smoothie)

Instructions:

1. Brew hibiscus tea by steeping the dried hibiscus flowers in hot water for about 5-10 minutes. Let it cool down before using.
2. In a blender, combine the raspberries, banana, brewed hibiscus tea (strained and cooled), honey or agave syrup (if using), and coconut water or water.
3. Optionally, add a handful of ice cubes to the blender for a colder and thicker smoothie.
4. Blend all the ingredients together until smooth and creamy.
5. Taste the smoothie and adjust the sweetness by adding more honey or agave syrup if desired.
6. If the smoothie is too thick, add more coconut water or water gradually until you reach your desired consistency.
7. Once blended to your liking, pour the Raspberry Hibiscus smoothie into glasses.
8. Optionally, garnish with a fresh raspberry or a hibiscus flower on top for presentation.
9. Serve immediately and enjoy this unique and refreshing smoothie! The combination of raspberries and hibiscus offers a delightful blend of flavors that's perfect for a light and floral drink. Adjust sweetness and consistency to suit your preference.

www.ingramcontent.com/pod-product-compliance
Lightning Source LLC
LaVergne TN
LVHW081503060526
838201LV00056BA/2915